www.barefootmeandering.com

veritas • gnaritas • libertas

Aspiring
Workbook
Slant Cursive

English Lessons Through Literature

Happy Thought
By Robert Louis Stevenson

The world is so full of a number of things,
I'm sure we should all be as happy as kings.

Peter sat down to rest.

Now this riddle is

as old as the hills.

The Tale of Squirrel Nutkin

The tailor worked

and worked.

Old Mr. Bunny had no

opinion whatever of cats.

The Tale of Benjamin Bunny

Then Mrs. Tiggy-
winkle made tea.

But Mr. Jeremy liked

getting his feet wet.

The Tale of Mr. Jeremy Fisher

The Frogs and the Ox

"He had a sack with

something alive in it."

The Tale of Mr. Tod

"I can see the marks

of little dirty feet."

"When it rains, I

sit in my little

sandy burrow."

The Tale of Johnny Town-mouse

What a sight met

the eyes of Jane

and Lucinda!

"One, two, three,

four, five, six little

fat rabbits!"

The Tale of the Flopsy Bunnies

She thought that it
looked a safe quiet spot.

The Spendthrift and the Swallow

Miss Moppet jumps

upon the Mouse!

"Let us climb up the

rockery," said Moppet.

The Tale of Tom Kitten

"I shall after supper,"

said Pig-wig.

"Who's been digging

up my nuts?"

The Tale of Timmy Tiptoes

"Which way did
she go, Moppet?"

" Shall I run for

the doctor? "

The Pie and the Patty-pan

The Birds, the Beasts, and the Bat

The Falling Star
By Sara Teasdale

I saw a star slide down the sky,
Blinding the north as it went by,
Too burning and too quick to hold,
Too lovely to be bought or sold,
Good only to make wishes on
And then forever to be gone.

"This is the last
straw," said Pickles.

The Falling Star
By Sara Teasdale

I saw a star slide down the sky,
Blinding the north as it went by,
Too burning and too quick to hold,
Too lovely to be bought or sold,
Good only to make wishes on
And then forever to be gone.

I saw a star slide

down the sky,

He does not say,

" Please. " He takes it!

"No," said the Whale.

"What is it like?"

"Come out and trot
like the rest of us."

The Falling Star
By Sara Teasdale

I saw a star slide down the sky,
Blinding the north as it went by,
Too burning and too quick to hold,
Too lovely to be bought or sold,
Good only to make wishes on
And then forever to be gone.

Blinding the north

as it went by,

It tickled like cake

crumbs in bed.

And Baviaan

winked. He knew.

Just So Stories: How the Leopard Got His Spots

The Eagle and the Jackdaw

"Come hither, Little

One," said the Crocodile.

Just So Stories: The Elephant's Child

The Falling Star
By Sara Teasdale

I saw a star slide down the sky,
Blinding the north as it went by,
Too burning and too quick to hold,
Too lovely to be bought or sold,
Good only to make wishes on
And then forever to be gone.

Too burning and too

quick to hold,

"Do you see that

gentleman dancing

on an ash pit?"

Just So Stories: The Sing-Song of Old Man Kangaroo

And he had a friend,

a slow-solid Tortoise.

Now attend and listen!

Just So Stories: How the First Letter Was Written

The Falling Star
By Sara Teasdale

I saw a star slide down the sky,
Blinding the north as it went by,
Too burning and too quick to hold,
Too lovely to be bought or sold,
Good only to make wishes on
And then forever to be gone.

Too lovely to be

bought or sold,

Her Daddy said, "Don't

be silly, child."

Just So Stories: How the Alphabet Was Made

"Was that well

done?" said the

Eldest Magician.

The Eagle and the Beetle

"And if you say three
words?" said the Cat.

The Falling Star
By Sara Teasdale

I saw a star slide down the sky,
Blinding the north as it went by,
Too burning and too quick to hold,
Too lovely to be bought or sold,
Good only to make wishes on
And then forever to be gone.

Good only to make

wishes on

And he held out his

finger and said, "Little

man, come here."

"Don't you know a

sand-fairy when

you see one?"

Five Children and It, Chapter 1

"Don't you forget,

it won't last

after sunset."

The Falling Star
By Sara Teasdale

I saw a star slide down the sky,
Blinding the north as it went by,
Too burning and too quick to hold,
Too lovely to be bought or sold,
Good only to make wishes on
And then forever to be gone.

And then forever

to be gone.

"It doesn't matter,"

said Robert sulkily.

"Oh, this isn't a

magic wish."

The Milkmaid and Her Pail

How Many Days
A Mother Goose Rhyme

How many days has my baby to play?
Saturday, Sunday, Monday,
Tuesday, Wednesday, Thursday, Friday,
Saturday, Sunday, Monday.

"You won't believe us,

but it doesn't matter."

How Many Days
A Mother Goose Rhyme

How many days has my baby to play?
Saturday, Sunday, Monday,
Tuesday, Wednesday, Thursday, Friday,
Saturday, Sunday, Monday.

How many days has

my baby to play?

"It's just like that

sand-fairy!"

Actions speak louder

than words.

Maxim

"And I'll tell the

others to fetch theirs."

"We're wasting the

whole morning."

Five Children and It, Chapter 8

How Many Days
A Mother Goose Rhyme

How many days has my baby to play?
Saturday, Sunday, Monday,
Tuesday, Wednesday, Thursday, Friday,
Saturday, Sunday, Monday.

Saturday, Sunday,

Monday,

"Let's wake him up

and see what he'll do."

Five Children and It, Chapter 9

Practice makes perfect.

"Don't be silly.

It's a matter of

life and death."

The Hares and the Frogs

"Goodness knows what

we're in for!"

Five Children and It, Chapter 11

How Many Days
A Mother Goose Rhyme

How many days has my baby to play?
Saturday, Sunday, Monday,
Tuesday, Wednesday, Thursday, Friday,
Saturday, Sunday, Monday.

Tuesday, Wednesday,

Thursday, Friday,

"Enter, then, and look,"

said Father Wolf stiffly.

Many hands make

light work.

Maxim

"He is a man—

a man—a man!"

snarled the Pack.

The Jungle Book: Mowgli's Brothers

"But think how

small he is," said

the Black Panther.

How Many Days
A Mother Goose Rhyme

How many days has my baby to play?
Saturday, Sunday, Monday,
Tuesday, Wednesday, Thursday, Friday,
Saturday, Sunday, Monday.

Saturday, Sunday,

Monday.

"Is there yet light
enough to see?"

Waste not, want not.

Maxim

"Are all well in the

jungle?" said Mowgli,

hugging him.

The Lion and the Ass

Summer Days
By Christina Rossetti

Winter is cold-hearted;
Spring is yea and nay;
Autumn is a weathercock;
Blown every way:
Summer days for me
When every leaf is on its tree.

"Have I kept my word?" said Mowgli.

The Jungle Book: "Tiger! Tiger!"

Summer Days
By Christina Rossetti

Winter is cold-hearted;
Spring is yea and nay;
Autumn is a weathercock;
Blown every way:
Summer days for me
When every leaf is on its tree.

Winter is

cold-hearted;

"Look at me!"

The Jungle Book: The White Seal

Think before you speak.

Maxim

" Look out for

yourselves!"

The Jungle Book: The White Seal

"What is the matter?"

asked Rikki-tikki.

Summer Days
By Christina Rossetti

Winter is cold-hearted;
Spring is yea and nay;
Autumn is a weathercock;
Blown every way:
Summer days for me
When every leaf is on its tree.

Spring is yea

and nay;

But he did not

grow too proud.

Let sleeping dogs lie.

Maxim

"Yes," said Little

Toomai, "he is

afraid of me."

The Mischievous Dog

"The child speaks

truth," said he.

Summer Days
By Christina Rossetti

Winter is cold-hearted;
Spring is yea and nay;
Autumn is a weathercock;
Blown every way:
Summer days for me
When every leaf is on its tree.

Autumn is a

weathercock;

"It's too dark to

see much."

A stitch in time

saves nine.

And the officer

answered, "An order

was given."

"Stop! You are tickling

me all over!"

Pinocchio, Chapters 1-2

Summer Days
By Christina Rossetti

Winter is cold-hearted;
Spring is yea and nay;
Autumn is a weathercock;
Blown every way:
Summer days for me
When every leaf is on its tree.

Blown every way.

"Tell me, Cricket,

who may you be?"

Pinocchio, Chapters 3-4

Curiosity killed the cat.

Maxim

"Would you be kind

enough to give me

a little bread?"

The Fox and the Lion

"Open the door,

I tell you!"

Pinocchio, Chapters 7-8

Summer Days
By Christina Rossetti

Winter is cold-hearted;
Spring is yea and nay;
Autumn is a weathercock;
Blown every way:
Summer days for me
When every leaf is on its tree.

summer days for me

He stopped and listened.

April showers bring

May flowers.

Maxim

"How do you come to

know my name?"

asked the puppet.

Pinocchio, Chapters 11-12

The next day Fire Eater
called Pinocchio aside.

"give ear to me, and

go back, my boy."

Summer Days
By Christina Rossetti

Winter is cold-hearted;
Spring is yea and nay;
Autumn is a weathercock;
Blown every way:
Summer days for me
When every leaf is on its tree.

When every leaf

is on its tree.

"Good morning, Pinocchio,"

said the fox.

"How do you know my name?"

asked the marionette.

"You shall not escape

from us again!"

Virtue is its

own reward.

Maxim

He saw a little cottage gleaming

white as the snow among

the trees of the forest.

"My boy, you will

repent it."

The Wolf and the Sheep

Snow Song
By Sara Teasdale

Fairy snow, fairy snow,
Blowing, blowing everywhere,
Would that I
Too, could fly
Lightly, lightly through the air.

"What a good Fairy you

are," said the puppet, "and

how much I love you!"

Snow Song
By Sara Teasdale

Fairy snow, fairy snow,
Blowing, blowing everywhere,
Would that I
Too, could fly
Lightly, lightly through the air.

Fairy snow,

fairy snow,

"I will never do

it again."

A penny saved is

a penny earned.

Maxim

Pinocchio was awakened by sounds from the yard. He stuck his nose out of the doghouse.

"Oh, little Fairy,

why did you die?"

The jug was very heavy, and

Pinocchio, not being strong

enough to carry it with his hands,

had to put it on his head.

"But you cannot grow,"

replied the Fairy.

Pinocchio, Chapters 25-26

Snow Song
By Sara Teasdale

Fairy snow, fairy snow,
Blowing, blowing everywhere,
Would that I
Too, could fly
Lightly, lightly through the air.

Blowing, Blowing

everywhere,

Pinocchio makes a promise to the

fairy. His wish is to be a real boy.

"Really," said the

puppet, "you make me

inclined to laugh."

Better late than never.

Maxim

"Open your eyes, Eugene! How shall I ever go home now? Why did I listen to those boys?"

"Is the Fairy at home?"

asked the puppet.

Pinocchio, Chapters 29-30

The Dogs and the Fox

"I intend to

study, as all well

conducted boys do."

Pinocchio, Chapters 31-32

Snow Song
By Sara Teasdale

Fairy snow, fairy snow,
Blowing, blowing everywhere,
Would that I
Too, could fly
Lightly, lightly through the air.

Would that I

And do you know what

this sea-monster was?

Pinocchio, Chapters 33-34

Honesty is the

best policy.

Maxim

"I swear I shall never again taste fish."

"Papa, help me,

I am dying!"

"Lean on my arm, dear Father, and let us go. We will walk very, very slowly."

"The trap caught me and the Farmer put a collar on me and made me a watchdog."

"The new one is the

best of all," said

the children.

Snow Song
By Sara Teasdale

Fairy snow, fairy snow,
Blowing, blowing everywhere,
Would that I
Too, could fly
Lightly, lightly through the air.

Too, could fly

"Did you ever see anything quite as ugly as that great tall creature? He is a disgrace to any brood. I shall go and chase him out!"

"That is our secret,"

said the doves.

Penny wise,

pound foolish.

"I have dropped my axe in the

forest. Bid your daughter go and

fetch it, for mine has worked hard

all day and is both wet and weary."

"Well, I must take

the cat with me,"

answered the bird.

The Lion and the Ass

"I wish to see his

Majesty," said he.

Snow Song
By Sara Teasdale

Fairy snow, fairy snow,
Blowing, blowing everywhere,
Would that I
Too, could fly
Lightly, lightly through the air.

Lightly, lightly

through the air.

"I am rich enough already," she

answered, "but I am often dull, and

I think you may amuse me a little."

∿∿∿∿∿

Once upon a time there lived

a king who was always at

war with his neighbors.

"Take me," it said in

a gentle whisper, and

all will go well."

Charity begins at home.

It was not until they were

galloping breathlessly towards

the palace that the princess knew

that she was taken captive.

"My good or evil fortune,"

replied the boy, "I

know not which."

When they heard the story of

the crystal cradle, they sat upright

and looked at each other.

〰〰〰

"And when the children are grown

up, they can return to their father

and set their mother free."

Rain
By Robert Louis Stevenson

The rain is raining all around,
It falls on field and tree,
It rains on the umbrellas here,
And on the ships at sea.

"And you really think

you can cure me?"

asked the king.

The Orange Fairy Book: The White Slipper

Rain
By Robert Louis Stevenson

The rain is raining all around,
It falls on field and tree,
It rains on the umbrellas here,
And on the ships at sea.

The rain is raining

all around,

He snatched it from the case and

thrust his foot into it, nearly weeping

for joy when he found he could walk

and run as easily as any beggar boy.

And while he is on his way let us pause

for a moment and tell who he is.

"Little Rabbit," she

said, "don't you

know who I am?"

still waters run deep.

Maxim

For a long time he lived in the toy cupboard or on the nursery floor, and no one thought very much about him.

~~~~~~~~

The velveteen rabbit was naturally shy, and being only made of velveteen, some of the more expensive toys quite snubbed him.

"Sh! Violet! Come!"

The Box-Car Children, Chapter 1

The Two Goats

"What's the matter?"

demanded Henry.

The Box-Car Children, Chapter 2

Rain
By Robert Louis Stevenson

The rain is raining all around,
It falls on field and tree,
It rains on the umbrellas here,
And on the ships at sea.

It falls on field

and tree,

She looked in every direction for

shelter. She even walked quite

a little way into the woods and

down a hill. And there she stood,

not knowing what to do next.

"I will get in, and you

hand him up to me."

"I've found a place!

Hurry! Hurry!"

We can do more good

by being good than

in any other way.

Maxim

The dog lifted his eyes and wagged his

tail feebly. He held up his front foot.

~~~~~~

"Poor doggie," murmured

Jess soothingly as she

clambered out of the car.

"I'm sorry we haven't

cups," Jess remarked.

The Box-Car Children, Chapter 4

"Wet my handkerchief,"

Jess ordered briskly.

But you should have seen him stare

when he saw what she was holding!

"It's delicious!" declared

Jess. "Cold as ice."

The Box-Car Children, Chapter 5

Rain
By Robert Louis Stevenson

The rain is raining all around,
It falls on field and tree,
It rains on the umbrellas here,
And on the ships at sea.

It rains on the
umbrellas here,

This was the strangest spot of all,

for behind the little waterfall was a

small quiet pool in which Jess had set

the milk bottles the night before.

Milk suited Benny very well, however,

so the older children allowed him to

drink rather more than his share.

"Well, why couldn't it wire,

Henry?" struck in Jess.

Once bitten, twice shy.

"These are trick spoons," explained Henry.

"I wonder if we couldn't fix up a regular swimming pool," he said.

"You just build it, and

you'll see later."

The Box-Car Children, Chapter 7

"You just build it, and

you'll see later."

The Box-Car Children, Chapter 7

The Leap at Rhodes

"You can actually

swim a few strokes

in it, Jess."

The Box-Car Children, Chapter 8

And on the

ships at sea.

It was a hollow about three yards

across. There were no stones in it at all.

The two older children dragged

all the logs while Violet and

Benny attended to the stones.

"What did it smell

like?" inquired Benny.

A good beginning

makes a good ending.

Maxim

Even the merry little brook

looked deserted.

~~~~~~~~~

"You see, this is a cherry year, and

we have to work quickly when we

once begin. Perhaps he could fill the

small baskets from the big ones."

"It's fun to run,

anyhow," he thought.

The Box-Car Children, Chapter 10

Henry was washing the concrete

drives at Dr. McAllister's house.

The man tossed him a pair of white

shoes and some blue trunks.

If You See a Tiny Fairy
By William Shakespeare

If you see a tiny fairy,
Lying fast asleep
Shut your eyes
And run away,
Do not stay to peek!
Do not tell
Or you'll break a fairy spell.

"Don't you see,

Benny?" Jess

explained patiently.

If You See a Tiny Fairy
By William Shakespeare

If you see a tiny fairy,
Lying fast asleep
Shut your eyes
And run away,
Do not stay to peek!
Do not tell
Or you'll break a fairy spell.

If you see a tiny fairy,

"He left it for over forty

years, you see."

Henry always insisted that

the rat's tail was too long.

"Ginseng?" echoed

Benny, thinking deeply.

"That's a nice name."

The Box-Car Children, Chapter 12

The early bird

catches the worm.

It was about a foot high with branching

leaves and a fine feathery white flower.

One day Jess began

to teach Benny a

little arithmetic.

The Plane Tree

"Couldn't I see them?"

begged the man,

almost like a boy.

If You See a Tiny Fairy
By William Shakespeare

If you see a tiny fairy,
Lying fast asleep
Shut your eyes
And run away,
Do not stay to peek!
Do not tell
Or you'll break a fairy spell.

Lying fast asleep

Shut your eyes

But something in the man's last
sentence rang in Henry's ears.

"I didn't know,

Benny," said Jess,

turning pink.

The Box-Car Children, Chapter 15

An apple a day keeps
the doctor away.

Maxim

"I hid behind the big white

rock with the flat top."

~~~~~~~~~~

But her grandfather did

not seem to mind.

They ate chicken sandwiches on

the very same tablecloth, and

Benny drank from his pink cup.

"Do you live all
alone, Grandfather?"
asked Benny.

"He is the dog, all right. He knows me,

as you see. His name is Rough No. 3.

He has a black spot inside his ear."

~~~~~~~~~~

The big car purred along from

Greenfield to Townsend in no time.

"And what am I
going to do?" asked
Jess, curiously.

If You See a Tiny Fairy
By William Shakespeare

If you see a tiny fairy,
Lying fast asleep
Shut your eyes
And run away,
Do not stay to peek!
Do not tell
Or you'll break a fairy spell.

And run away,

Do not stay to peek!

Here the rooms were not quite so large. They were sunny and homelike.

~~~~~~~~~

"But we never could have done it without Watch. He stayed and looked after them while I was away, and he just thinks everything of Jess."

"I am going away
to hunt," said the
king one morning.

The Orange Fairy Book: How Ian Direach Got the Blue Falcon

Birds of a feather

flock together.

And in his dream a soft nose touched

him, and a warm body curled up beside

him, and a low voice whispered to him.

〰〰〰〰〰〰〰

With that Ian Direach awoke and

beheld Gille Mairtean the fox.

"Have you no pity

for a poor mother?"

asked the fox.

The Sheep and the Pig

"You sold your dead

wife?" cried the people.

If You See a Tiny Fairy
By William Shakespeare

If you see a tiny fairy,
Lying fast asleep
Shut your eyes
And run away,
Do not stay to peek!
Do not tell
Or you'll break a fairy spell.

Do not tell

Every evening the goldsmith walked

across to the cowherd's house and

said, "Come. Let's go out for a walk!'

~~~~~~~

"Why, down in that place in the river

where you threw me in, I found

meadows, and trees, and fine pastures,

and buffalo, and all kinds of cattle."

Just as he spoke, there

came a double knock

at the house door.

To be good is the
mother of to do good.

He turned and turned, and the

roast got nice and brown.

He did not, of course, agree

particularly well with his brothers, or,

rather, they did not agree with him.

"Bless me, what's

that?" exclaimed

Gluck, jumping up.

The thought was agreed to be
a very good one; they hired a
furnace and turned goldsmiths.

"Suppose we turn goldsmiths,"
said Schwartz to Hans as they
entered the large city.

"Water!" he stretched

his arms to Hans

and cried feebly.

If You See a Tiny Fairy
By William Shakespeare

If you see a tiny fairy,
Lying fast asleep,
Shut your eyes
And run away,
Do not stay to peek!
Do not tell
Or you'll break a fairy spell.

Or you'll break

a fairy spell.

His way now lay straight up a
ridge of bare red rocks.

"Three drops are enough," he thought.

"I may, at least, cool my lips with it."

But the thirst for gold

prevailed over his fear,

and he rushed on.

The King of the Golden River, Chapter 4

Good things come to
those who wait.

Maxim

But Gluck was very sorry

and cried all night.

~~~~~~~~~~

And when Schwartz stood by the

brink of the Golden River, its waves

were black like thunder clouds,

but their foam was like fire.

"Oh dear me!" said

Gluck. "Have you

really been so cruel?"

The Lion, the Bear, and the Fox

Made in the USA
Monee, IL
30 July 2022

10580542R00129